Martin Luther King Jr.

Dona Herweck

Consultant

Timothy Rasinski, Ph.D.
Kent State University

Publishing Credits

Dona Herweck Rice, *Editor-in-Chief*
Robin Erickson, *Production Director*
Lee Aucoin, *Creative Director*
Conni Medina, M.A.Ed., *Editorial Director*
Jamey Acosta, *Editor*
Stephanie Reid, *Photo Editor*
Rachelle Cracchiolo, M.S.Ed., *Publisher*

Based on writing from *TIME For Kids*.

TIME For Kids and the *TIME For Kids* logo are registered trademarks of TIME Inc. Used under license.

Teacher Created Materials

5301 Oceanus Drive
Huntington Beach, CA 92649-1030
http://www.tcmpub.com

ISBN 978-1-4333-3641-6

© 2012 Teacher Created Materials, Inc.

Table of Contents

Unfair!

Martin came home one day feeling sad. His good friend would not play with him. The boy's father told him not to play with Martin because Martin had dark skin.

Martin's parents hugged him. They told him about **unfair** things that happened to them, too, because of their skin color. They said that sometimes fear and hatred make people do terrible things.

drinking fountain for African Americans

What Are Civil Rights?

Civil rights are freedoms given to all citizens, such as freedom of speech, freedom to vote, and freedom to assemble peacefully.

Martin knew these things were wrong. He wanted to make things better. He said, "I'm going to turn this world upside down."

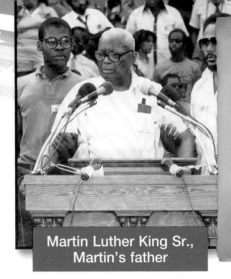

Martin Luther King Sr.,
Martin's father

Martin grew up to be Dr. Martin Luther King Jr., the great **civil rights** leader. And he did turn the world upside down.

Where Love Was Central

Martin Luther King Jr. was born on January 15, 1929, in Atlanta, Georgia. Martin's home was happy. He and his sister, Christine, and brother, A.D., felt love all around them. Martin wrote that his home was a place "where love was central."

Christine and Adam Daniel (A.D.), Martin's siblings

birthplace of Martin Luther King Jr.

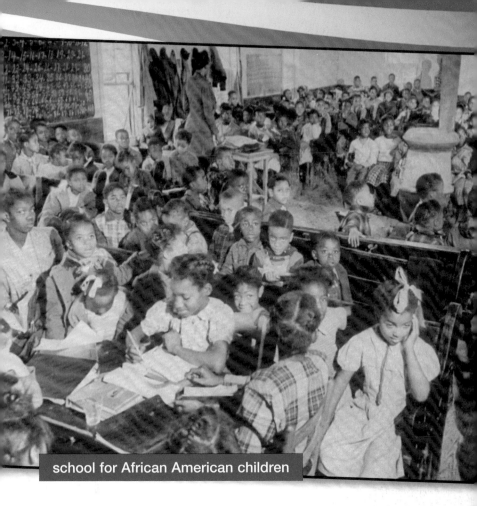

school for African American children

But the world outside Martin's home was not always filled with love. **African Americans** were not allowed the same rights as other people. They suffered because of other people's hatred and fear.

Once when Martin was 15, he was riding a full bus. Some white people got on, and Martin had to give them his seat. He rode the bus for 90 minutes standing up. He was so angry!

African Americans had to sit at the back of the bus.

The law said that Martin had to give up his seat, but the law was unfair and unjust.

Growing Up

school desegregation, 1957

Martin's father was a **Baptist minister**, and his mother, Alberta, was a teacher and musician. Martin's father went to college, even though few African Americans then had a chance to go.

Martin's parents taught him by their example. They never shopped where they were treated badly, and they worked hard to end **segregation**.

Segregation

Segregation is separating people by their skin color and keeping all the public things they can use, such as bathrooms, drinking fountains, movie theaters, and schools separate. Very often, what African Americans were given to use was not as good as what other people had.

Martin was smart. He skipped two grades and started college young.

Martin was a talented speaker, too. One speech he gave in school was about

Love for Books

Martin loved to read, and he spent a lot of time doing it. His father said, "He kept books around him. He just liked the idea of having them."

slavery in the United States. He said it was especially wrong because Americans believe all people "are created free and equal."

Ministry

Theology

Theology is the study of God and religion. To be a doctor means to have studied so much that a person becomes a top expert in that area. A doctor who helps sick people is a top expert in medicine. A doctor of theology is a top expert in God and religion.

Martin went to Morehouse College in Atlanta. He then went to a college in Boston to become a minister, and a third college to become a doctor of theology. When he graduated, he became Dr. King.

In Boston, Martin met a music student named Coretta Scott. They were married and had four children.

After college, Martin began work as a minister. Later, he joined his father as **pastor** of Ebenezer Baptist Church in Atlanta.

Coretta Scott King and Bernice, Martin's daughter

In college, Martin heard about Mohandas Gandhi (mo-HAN-dis GAHN-dee). Gandhi worked to free India from Great Britain's rule, but he did not start a war to do it. He led peaceful **marches** and **boycotts**. He broke unfair laws. Gandhi was often **arrested**

Gandhi

Mohandas Gandhi died in 1948. He is remembered today as one of the most important leaders of nonviolent social change. So is Dr. King.

Resistance

A march is a large parade of people who walk together to bring attention to a problem they care about. A boycott happens when a group of people will not use or buy something until the wrong things about it are changed.

and threatened, but he kept working peacefully until India was free.

Martin liked Gandhi's ideas. He decided to do the same things to help free African Americans from unfair laws and bad treatment.

Civil Rights

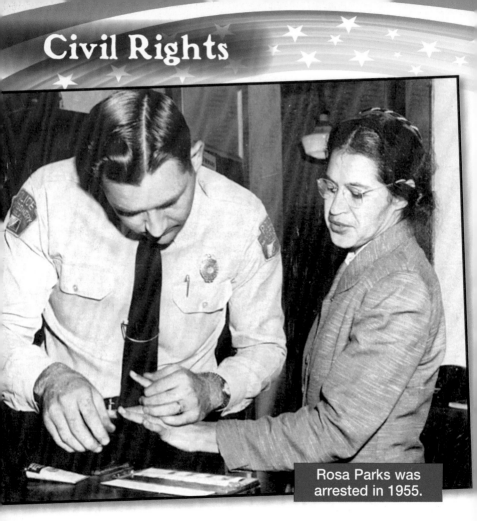

Rosa Parks was arrested in 1955.

On December 1, 1955, Rosa Parks was riding a full bus in Montgomery, Alabama. When white people got on the bus, she was told to give up her seat. She said no, so police arrested her.

Martin proudly rode the first desegregated bus after the Supreme Court decision.

Martin was asked to lead a boycott of Montgomery buses. Many African Americans chose not to ride them for many months. Finally, the **United States Supreme Court** said it was illegal to segregate buses.

Martin led many causes in the Civil Rights Movement. He marched and gave speeches. Martin was arrested and threatened many times. Once, he was stabbed and nearly died. His house was bombed, too. But Martin just said, "We must meet hate with love." He kept on marching and **preaching** about peace and **nonviolence**.

Martin Luther King Jr.
arrested in 1960

March on Washington

In 1963, about 250,000 people marched to **Washington, DC** to talk about freedom. It was called the March on Washington. Martin gave his famous "I Have a Dream" speech there. He talked about his dream that one day all people would join together in peace and freedom.

Fifty thousand people followed Martin's coffin on the way to Morehouse College where he was buried.

Martin saw many good changes in his life, but he did not live to see the day he dreamed about. On April 4, 1968, he was shot and killed while speaking from his motel balcony in Memphis, Tennessee. He was only 39 years old.

The night before he died, Martin gave a speech and said he was not worried about death. He knew the "promised land" was coming, a place where all of his dreams would come true.

Martin's birthday is now a national holiday. Almost every major city around the country has a school, park, or street named after him. The King Center in Atlanta helps to continue Martin's work for civil justice for all people through nonviolence.

Martin Luther King Jr. is a true American hero. He did, indeed, turn the world upside down.

Martin Luther King Jr. Time Line

1929	born in Atlanta on January 15
1944	started college at age 15
1948	graduated from Morehouse College
1953	**married Coretta Scott** ••••••••••••••
1955	• graduated with doctorate from Boston University • **led the Montgomery bus boycott from December 1955 to December 1956** ••••••••••••••••
1956	became involved in the Civil Rights Movement
1960	joined his father as pastor of Ebenezer Baptist Church
1963	**led the March on Washington on August 28** ••••••••••••••••••••••••
1964	• won Nobel Peace Prize (youngest person ever) • Civil Rights Bill made segregation illegal
1965	**Voting Rights Act signed by President Johnson** ••••••••••••
1968	killed in Memphis, Tennessee on April 4 at age 39
1986	birthday became a national holiday

Glossary

African Americans—the citizens of the United States whose ancestors came from Africa

arrested—taken by the police, charged with a crime, and placed in jail

Baptist—a Christian religion

boycott—to not buy from or give business to

civil rights—the freedoms given to all citizens

marches—large parades of people who walk together to bring attention to a problem they care about

minister—a person who leads others in their religious or spiritual life

nonviolence—peacefully resistant

pastor—a minister who is in charge of a church

preaching—speaking in a serious way about right and wrong, usually done by a minister

segregation—separating people by their skin color and keeping all the public things they can use separate

unfair—not equal for everyone

United States Supreme Court—the highest and most important court in the United States

Washington, DC—the capital of the United States